Tales from the Crypts

Exploring the World's Hidden Tombs

Table of Contents

1. Introduction 1

2. The Enigma of Egypt: The Valley of the Kings 2

    2.1. The Saga Begins 2

    2.2. The Construction of the Tombs 2

    2.3. The Withholding of Time: Notable Tombs in the Valley 3

    2.4. Archaeological Adventures: Recent Discoveries 3

    2.5. Concluding Musings 4

3. Paris Catacombs: The Empire of the Dead 5

    3.1. The Origin of the Catacombs 5

    3.2. Discovery and Exploration 6

    3.3. The Empire of the Dead 6

    3.4. Cataphiles and Modern Exploration 7

4. Mausoleum of the First Qin Emperor: China's Terracotta Army 9

    4.1. The Origin Story 9

    4.2. Life in Death: The Terracotta Army 9

    4.3. Inside the Emperor's Tomb 10

    4.4. Conservation and Tourism Efforts 11

5. Sutton Hoo – Unveiling the Anglo-Saxon Legacy 12

    5.1. Sutton Hoo: The Discovery 12

    5.2. Unearthing Regal Riches 12

    5.3. The Man behind the Mask: An Anglo Saxon King? 13

    5.4. Sutton Hoo: A Time Machine to the Anglo-Saxon World 14

    5.5. Legacy of Sutton Hoo 14

6. Westminster Abbey Crypts: In the Heart of British monarchy 16

    6.1. The Story of Westminster Abbey 16

    6.2. Housing the Royals - The Regal Crypts 17

    6.3. The Poet's Corner 17

    6.4. The Tomb of the Unknown Warrior 18

7. The Pharaohs of Sudan: Pyramids of the Black Kingdom 19

   7.1. Relics of Kush 19

      7.1.1. Worship and Burial 19

      7.1.2. Architecture and Significance 20

   7.2. Explorations and Excavations 20

      7.2.1. Reisner's Work 20

      7.2.2. Further Excavations 20

   7.3. Looking Past the Sandstorms 21

      7.3.1. Defying Time and Nature 21

      7.3.2. Identity and Legacy 21

8. Newgrange – Reviving Ireland's Ancient Astronomic Marvel . . . 23

   8.1. The Discovery 23

   8.2. Description of the Monument 23

   8.3. Astronomical and Mythological Significance 24

   8.4. Excavation and Preservation 24

   8.5. Closing Thoughts 25

9. St.Peter's Tomb: A Journey Beneath the Vatican City 26

   9.1. The Invisible Basilica 26

   9.2. The Excavations Unearthed 26

   9.3. The Rediscovery 27

   9.4. In the Shadow of the Pope 27

   9.5. Skeptics and Believers 28

   9.6. A Symbol of Unwavering Faith 28

10. Taj Mahal: The Crypt of Eternal Love 30

   10.1. Traversing Through Time 30

   10.2. The Man and His Muse 30

   10.3. A Masterpiece in Marble 31

   10.4. The Crypt of Eternal Love 31

   10.5. The Untamed Beauty of the Gardens 32

   10.6. A Love Story Engraved in Stone 32

11. The Capuchin Crypt: Rome's Chapel of Bones 34

    11.1. Origins and Construction 34

    11.2. Design and Decorum 34

    11.3. Reflections on Life and Death 35

    11.4. Contemporary Reverence 36

Chapter 1. Introduction

Dive into an adventurous realm where the past intertwines with the present and mystery shrouds every step you take! Our Special Report, "Tales from the Crypts: Exploring the World's Hidden Tombs," promises an uncanny yet intriguing journey through the hidden corners of the world's most enigmatic tombs, crypts, and cemeteries. This remarkable narrative, brimming with bone-chilling anecdotes, thrilling escapades, and reflections of civilizations lost in time, is sure to leave you on the edge of your seat, hungry for more. Whether you're a fervent history aficionado or a dazzling daredevil drawn to the supernatural, the riveting tales captured in this comprehensive report will kindle your curiosity and fire up your imagination. Get ready to embark on this spine-tingling voyage and unravel the mysteries that lie beneath the stone and earth. Secure your copy today!

Chapter 2. The Enigma of Egypt: The Valley of the Kings

Today, we commence our journey in the land of the pharaohs, a place steeped in ancient legends and impressive architectural grandeur. Here, in Egypt, the resting place of powerful rulers blurs the line between history and mythology; our destination: The Valley of the Kings.

2.1. The Saga Begins

It is here that the saga begins, a sprawling necropolis nestled in the rugged peaks of Deir el-Bahari, on the banks of the Nile. Designated a World Heritage Site in 1979, the Valley has served as a silent guardian of Egypt's most famous rulers and their opulent treasures for over three millennia.

The allure of The Valley lies not only in its majestic tombs and exquisite wall paintings but also in the mysteries that shroud its centuries-old corridors. A significant number of tombs have yet to be exposed, lying silently, waiting for the right time to narrate their tales of splendor and melancholy.

2.2. The Construction of the Tombs

To understand the extent of the mysteries surrounding The Valley, we must embark upon an exploration of its daunting construction process. The scale of dedication and craftsmanship evident in these structures is nothing less than awe-inspiring. These edifices, dug into the limestone, were meticulously carved and assembled by thousands of workers over several years.

What follows the construction of these crypts is an elaborate process of decoration that is a testament to the unparalleled talent of ancient Egyptian artisans. Frescoes come alive on the tomb walls, depicting scenes from the pharaoh's life, prayers to the gods, and complex symbols that were significant to the Egyptian's belief in life after death.

2.3. The Withholding of Time: Notable Tombs in the Valley

Among the many crypts in The Valley lays the tomb of Tutankhamun, the boy-king whose life and death are still enshrined in enigma. Discovered by British archaeologist Howard Carter in 1922, the treasure-filled tomb presents a vivid depiction of Egypt's prowess at art, culture, and funeral rites.

The tomb of Rameses V and VI is another spectacle, where grandeur multiplies with every step you take in the darkened corridors. Gigantic pillars and vibrant wall paintings beautifully encapsulate the riches and glory of the Middle Kingdom era.

Further, the tomb of Seti I, one of the best-preserved, stuns visitors with its captivating reliefs and hues. It presents a panoramic view of the underworld as visualised by the ancients, an unseen territory that certainly fires up one's imagination.

2.4. Archaeological Adventures: Recent Discoveries

The Valley continues to be a hotbed of archaeological undertakings as explorers keep making regular advances in unearthing its concealed narratives.

In the 21st century, discoveries like KV63 and KV64 have rewritten the understating of the enigma of Egypt's necropolis. Excavation of

KV63 uncovered seven coffins with a large collection of funerary remnants, while KV64 turned out to be the final resting place of a female chantress from the 22nd dynasty.

Similarly, the latest ground-penetrating radar investigation led by celebrated archaeologist Dr. Zahi Hawass suggests there might be unknown corridors leading from Tutankhamun's tomb. The astonishing possibility of lost burial chambers in the boy king's crypt has rekindled global interest in the enigma of The Valley.

2.5. Concluding Musings

Thus, the Valley of the Kings, with its mystic aura of the bygone era, paints a lucid picture of an ancient civilization obsessed with the concept of mortality and the afterlife. Each crypt in its vast expanse whispers thousand-year-old secrets, promising newer explorations, discoveries, and exciting revelations.

However, with recent advancements in archaeological technology, the concealed stories of these crypts are slowly rising from their deep slumber, inviting us to delve deeper and decode the ultimate mystery—life after death. As we peek behind the veil of time and pierce through the surface of the Valley, the golden mask of Tutankhamun reflects our faces in its ageless sheen, whispering "Curiosity feeds exploration."

Our quest into the realm of the crypts is far from over. Weaving through the corridors of the Valley, we stand at the cusp of understanding and mystery, ready to transport ourselves on a magic carpet ride across the continents and the epochs, one tomb at a time...

Chapter 3. Paris Catacombs: The Empire of the Dead

Underneath the bustling streets of the fashion capital of the world, Paris, a network of tunnels and chambers echoes a chilling tale of death and time - a world far removed from the city's grandeur and romance. The labyrinth of the Paris Catacombs, a veritable 'Empire of the Dead,' stretches over 200 miles, bisecting the French capital beneath the surface. In a city celebrated for its beauty, culture, and sophistication, the catacombs serve as a scintillating counterpoint, a grim reminder of mortality and history deeply interwoven into the city's fabric.

3.1. The Origin of the Catacombs

The story of the catacombs is intrinsically tied with the history of Paris itself. In the late 18th century, with the burial spaces across the city becoming overcrowded, disease-ridden, and noxious, the government was forced to make a difficult decision. Paris was dealing with a sanitation crisis that necessitated an urgent, radical solution. Being one of the largest cities globally, the increasing mortality meant the need for burial grounds surpassed available space.

In an innovative albeit eerie solution, authorities decided to use the city's ancient underground quarries. The limestone quarries lying beneath the city were an already existing labyrinth dating back to Roman times, which provided the raw materials that built Paris. The decision was taken to transport the remains of nearly six million people from the city's cemeteries into these quarries, thus rendering birth to the Paris Catacombs.

The massive operation to move the bones started at nightfall, under the cover of a procession that involved priests singing the service for the dead. This operation was so significant that it went on for decades, continuing even into the 19th century.

3.2. Discovery and Exploration

The catacombs remained a clandestine world for many years. However, during the French Revolution, the catacombs began to pique curiosity and became a symbol of the national heritage. The public interest started growing around the intricacies of its creation and its symbolic significance to Paris's history.

By the 19th century, the catacombs were officially opened to the public, and everyone, from nobles to proletariat, flocked to delve into the underworld. Their first encounter was the chilling entrance inscription, "Stop! Here lies the Empire of the Dead." This fascinating entanglement between history, morbidity, and thrill formed a desire to explore the crypts even further.

The catacombs have been visited by numerous historical figures, including Napoleon Bonaparte and Charles X. Ever the source of inspiration, they have stimulated numerous publications and been depicted in art and literature.

3.3. The Empire of the Dead

Descending to the catacombs, one leaves the City of Light behind and plunges 20 meters below to enter the City of Shadows, a vast ossuary housing the remains of millions. The ghastly embellishments and the neatly stacked bones arranged in a macabre symmetry go beyond the realms of being simply an underground cemetery. These catacombs tell a story the surface world has long forgotten.

In stark contrast to the symmetry of Parisian architecture, the catacombs present a chaos and randomness that is nothing less than haunting. Skulls and tibiae are arranged in repetitive patterns, adorning the walls in chillingly aesthetic mosaics. The tunnels are adorned with periodic tablets and plaques bearing phrases profound and dark, often in Latin or traditional French gothic font, further adding to the morbidity of the place.

Much of what the catacombs contain remains unseen by the general public. A significant fraction of this underground world is illegal to access and deemed unsafe by the authorities. Secrets abound in these forbidden sections known as the 'catacombs non aménagées.'

3.4. Cataphiles and Modern Exploration

Over the years, a subculture has grown around the catacombs. 'Cataphiles,' as they are fondly known, are urban explorers who venture beyond the legal confines of the catacombs to delve into the lesser-known parts, risking danger and the ire of the law. Equipped with maps drawn by previous explorers, they often look for new entrances or other secrets left to be discovered in the intricate tunnel system that forms this empire of the dead.

The advent of the internet and its role in connecting people around common interests has led to the formation of a global community of cataphiles. Modern explorers from across the world connect online to share their experiences, and some even organize 'cataphile' meetings for shared exploration.

In a city that breathes history and art at every corner, the catacombs stand out as a monument not only to the dead but also to the living. Equal parts history, art, and adventure, the catacombs of Paris continue to fascinate and terrify, embodying a narrative that is both macabre and captivating.

The catacombs are inseparable from Paris, symbolizing the city's continuous evolution - teaching us that beneath the city's vibrant and elegant present, lies an echo of its dark yesteryears. The Empire of the Dead continues to remind us that life and death are but two sides of the same coin. Here, in the catacombs, they are intertwined to narrate the chillingly beautiful tale of humanity itself.

Chapter 4. Mausoleum of the First Qin Emperor: China's Terracotta Army

As the sun dips below the horizon, painting the evening sky a warm orange, an eerie shadow stretches over the Lintong District, casting the sprawling necropolis in a mysterious shade. Here, under the vast undulating landscape of modern-day Xi'an, lies the eternal resting place of Qin Shi Huang, the First Emperor of China, and a hidden army, forever poised and ready for battle. This monumental testament to human achievement echoes a time of ambition, upheaval and the unification of a nation.

4.1. The Origin Story

The Mausoleum of the First Qin Emperor, Qinshi Huangdi, grand as it is mysterious, is a trove of archaeological wonders. Its origin story is one that goes back over two millennia. Born as Ying Zheng in 259 BCE, Qin Shi Huang unified the warring kingdoms of China in 221 BCE, reigning as its first emperor. His desire for a grand afterlife paved the way for this architectural marvel.

Qin Shi Huang laid the foundation for his mausoleum soon after acceding to the throne of Qin at the ripe age of 13. It took nearly 700,000 workers and 38 years to complete this labyrinthine crypt.

4.2. Life in Death: The Terracotta Army

The most famous component of the mausoleum, the Terracotta Army, was first discovered in 1974 by local farmers digging a well. This led to one of the greatest archaeological discoveries of the 20th century.

Constructed to serve the Emperor in his afterlife, the Terracotta Army is a sight to behold. The three pits, which hold the army, are teeming with a staggering number of life-sized terracotta warriors and horses. Offering an uncanny echo of reality, these statues are individually crafted, with distinct faces, clothing and even hairstyles, reflecting the diverse demographics of Qin's unified China.

Interestingly, while each of the estimated 8,000 soldiers was originally vividly painted in colors such as blue, green, red, white and black, exposure to air - for the first time in over 2000 years - caused the painted layers to peel and fade within minutes of being unearthed.

The combat formation of the warriors provides valuable insights into the military strategy of the time. The true-to-life chariots, arms and armor further emphasize Emperor Qin's remarkable attention to detail.

4.3. Inside the Emperor's Tomb

Directly beneath the tomb mound lies the burial chamber of Emperor Qin, unexcavated to this day. According to Sima Qian, a historian from the Han Dynasty, the tomb chamber is a simulated cosmos, replicating Qin Shi Huang's empire. The chamber reportedly has replicas of palaces and scenic towers, celestial bodies strewn on its ceilings and crossbow traps to deter tomb raiders. There are also rivers and seas recreated using mercury, made possible by the Emperor's fascination with the elixir of life.

Modern-day surveys have confirmed unusually high concentrations of mercury in the soil of the mound, corroborating these ancient claims.

4.4. Conservation and Tourism Efforts

The Mausoleum of the First Qin Emperor raises numerous questions of conservation. Despite the discovery of the site in the '70s, only 1% has been unearthed. Careful excavation is in progress to prevent further degradation of the relics caused by exposure to modern atmosphere.

The emergence of the Mausoleum as a tourist hub saw the construction of a museum covering the three pits of the Terracotta Army. UNESCO recognised the Mausoleum as a World Heritage Site in 1987, acknowledging its historical and cultural value to humanity.

This monumental necropolis elegantly demonstrates the might of a man who wished for eternal life and successfully manifested it through his grand Mausoleum. The Terracotta Army, silent and frozen in time for thousands of years, continues to stand guard, commemorating the life of China's first emperor who carved an indelible mark on the fabric of history.

Chapter 5. Sutton Hoo – Unveiling the Anglo-Saxon Legacy

Tucked away in the serene rolling hills of Suffolk, England, lies an archaeological site that has reshaped our understanding of Anglo-Saxon history. Famed for its magnificence and historical significance, Sutton Hoo is a stretch of land studded with a scatter of burial mounds, or 'hoo's, that offer an eerie yet captivating glance into the enigmatic world of the early Middle Ages.

5.1. Sutton Hoo: The Discovery

"Sutton Hoo? More like Sutton Who!" This likely would have been the response of most people before 1939. What seemed to be an ordinary parcel of land was transformed into an invaluable archaeological site when landowner Mrs. Edith Pretty employed local archaeologist Basil Brown to examine the curious mounds on her property.

Unbeknownst to them, Brown and his team were about to unravel a sensational discovery that would shed light on a period often cloaked in the shadows of history - the time of the Anglo-Saxons. As soon as they had excavated Mound 1, they stumbled upon the haunting imprint of a long-disintegrated wooden ship. Perfectly aligned for a river-facing burial, the colossal ship measured nearly 27 meters in length. The size itself bore testament to the fact that these weren't ordinary tombs, but vessels of an extraordinary ritual - a testament to an era when warrior-kings roamed the earth.

5.2. Unearthing Regal Riches

Central to the ship was a burial chamber filled to the brim with treasures of staggering craftsmanship. Gold and garnet jewelry, silverware, sumptuous textiles, relics of warfare, and even a lyre instrument - each artifact a tangible echo of the past.

The most famous artifact - the Sutton Hoo helmet - is a masterpiece of regal symbolism and intricate design. Heavily ornamented with tawny garnets and tin-plated motifs, its face mask is embellished with eyebrows and moustaches wrought from gilded copper alloy wires, culminating in intricate plaits knotted around a stylized dragon head. Thought to have been deliberately dismantled before burial, the helmet has been painstakingly reassembled, revealing not only a functional piece of war gear but also a piece de resistance of the era's craftsmanship.

5.3. The Man behind the Mask: An Anglo Saxon King?

The royal grandeur of the artifacts suggested that the occupant of the tomb was no less than a king. The interred was likely Raedwald, who died around 624 AD and was a potentate of the East Anglian kingdom, ruling over the people later known as the Angles. Descended from Wuffingas (Wolf-people), Raedwald was not merely a local chieftain but a Bretwalda - an overlord ruling over all of the southern English.

Given his historical standing and the dateline of the burial, Raedwald fits the profile of the Sutton Hoo interred. The burial highlights the syncretism of traditions of the time, with Christian symbols cohabitating with pagan deities among the grave goods - mirroring Raedwald's conversion to Christianity, yet his simultaneous tolerance of the old worship.

5.4. Sutton Hoo: A Time Machine to the Anglo-Saxon World

The discoveries from Sutton Hoo opened up exciting avenues to better understand the social and cultural continuum of Anglo-Saxon England. The assortment of goods from Byzantium, the Mediterranean, and beyond, stand testament to the cross-cultural contact and geopolitical clout of the buried royal. From the gold coins to the trove of domestic artifacts, we have been given a rare peek into the daily courtly life, trade routes, craftsmanship techniques, and even attire of the era.

5.5. Legacy of Sutton Hoo

The finds at Sutton Hoo prompted a paradigm shift in our comprehension of the so-called 'Dark Ages'. Sutton Hoo remains emblematic of a moment in time when old gave way to new, and ancient worship morphed into Christianity. Post-discovery, the site transformed into a physical and metaphorical bridge between the 7th century and the present, breathing life into the unvoiced narratives of our ancestors.

The world of Sutton Hoo, with its spectral ship and regal belongings seemingly suspended in time, is a poignant testament to Anglo-Saxon power and legacy. After decades of mystery and silence, this site continues to work its magic, engaging not just historians and archaeologists, but also countless enthusiasts drawn into its rich, evocative story carved on the canvas of history. Today, thanks to ongoing studies and the dedicated museum built on the site, the story of Sutton Hoo carries on, igniting our imagination and our insatiable quest to know more about our ancestors.

Thus, in every sense of the word, Sutton Hoo is not just a burial site. It is a tapestry of time, where tangibility meets legend, and the pieces

of history connect with the narrative of the present, continually
expanding our knowledge and appreciation of the rich tapestry of
human history.

Chapter 6. Westminster Abbey Crypts: In the Heart of British monarchy

Within the bustling metropolis of London, cast in the shadow of Big Ben and the Houses of Parliament, lies one of England's most sacred sites: Westminster Abbey. This awe-inspiring, centuries-old church houses within its depths a labyrinth of hallowed crypts, holding the stories of kings long passed, poets who shifted paradigms, and even the remains of the Unknown Warrior.

6.1. The Story of Westminster Abbey

The story of Westminster Abbey is multi-hued, packed with pagan origins, rising kingdoms, feuding royals, and more than a hint of scandal. The site upon which it stands was initially believed to hold a Roman temple dedicated to Apollo, while there's evidence that a church was established, around the seventh century, by the early Christian convert, Mellitus.

But the true genesis of Westminster Abbey is tied to King Edward the Confessor, who, towards the end of his rule in 1042-66, commissioned a grand palace and accompanying Abbey in the Romanesque style. The Abbey was to be the centerpiece of his new capital: the spiritual and political heart, where future monarchs would be crowned and interred. Thus, the hallowed depths of Westminster Abbey were born, the crypts shaping history as much as history shaped the crypts.

6.2. Housing the Royals - The Regal Crypts

The most significant function of Westminster Abbey's crypts has certainly been to house the remains of the monarchs, their consorts, kin, and most esteemed advisors. Yet, it's important to note that not all royalty have been venerated equally.

In the Chapel of St. Peter ad Vincula, one can find the notorious Henry VIII's most famous wives: Anne Boleyn and Catherine Howard. Their remains, accused of high treason, were hastily buried without any monumental inscription, a sharp contrast to the grandeur of the Royal Tombs.

At the core, the Royal Tombs are a testament to national memory and Kingship. Mary, Queen of Scots, for instance, was initially buried in Peterborough Cathedral but was later disinterred by her enthusiastic son, James I, who reburied his mother in an elaborate tomb opposite his arch-nemesis, Queen Elizabeth I. This act was an assertion of their equal status, irrespective of their political conflicts.

6.3. The Poet's Corner

Commencing with the burial of Geoffrey Chaucer in October 1400, the South Transept of the Abbey evolved into the famous "Poet's Corner." While not a crypt per se, this area beneath the Abbey forms part of the subterranean narrative, an underground celebration of art and intellect.

This corner hosts an elite group of literary luminaries, from the rustic bard William Shakespeare, whose monument bears his effigy but not his body, to industrialized Victorian-era authors such as Charles Dickens. Significantly, many who earn their memorial here are not physically present, a testament to the power of the metaphorical crypt.

6.4. The Tomb of the Unknown Warrior

An imposing black Belgian marble stone, bearing an inscription, and surrounded by poppies, marks the grave of an Unknown Warrior. Located near the west entrance of the Abbey, this tomb, inaugurated on November 11, 1920, represents the unidentified fallen of World War I.

"An unknown British warrior," the stone reads, "buried here on Armistice Day 1920, in the presence of His Majesty King George V, his ministers of state, the chiefs of his forces, and a vast concourse of the nation." The tomb embodies the collective mourning of a nation, a symbol of the immense human cost of war laid bare within the cryptic depth.

Westminster Abbey and its crypts bear tales of whispering stone and existential riddles of dusty royal bones. Yet, even now, it's not simply a sepulcher of the past. It persists as a venerated space that draws countless pilgrims who traverse its hallowed paths, seeking a glimpse of their distant ancestors or paying homage to heroes of yore. The echoes of the past persist, and the crypts of Westminster Abbey continue to be an essential part of our shared cultural legacy.

Chapter 7. The Pharaohs of Sudan: Pyramids of the Black Kingdom

In the midst of panoramic desert vistas stands an unmistakable testament to a civilization as grand, high-reaching, and enigmatic as the edifices themselves - the Pyramids of Nuri, Sudan. Shadowed long by their more renowned Egyptian counterparts, these mysterious granaries of the ancients unfurl a tale that ties the knot of the present with the strings of a past, an epoch buried deep under the burning sand.

7.1. Relics of Kush

Two millennia ago, the Kingdom of Kush, centered around the city of Meroe, flourished as an economic power and cultural crossroads. For nearly a thousand years, the empire held its ground, refusing to bow down to more powerful neighboring dynasties. The vestigial wonders that bear testament to this long overlooked civilization are the Nubian pyramids, erected as the final resting place for its royal generations.

7.1.1. Worship and Burial

The Kushite rulers held an indomitable belief in life after death, following the tradition of the Pharaohs of the North. Thus arose the tradition of erecting pyramids, encapsulating both their devout worship of the gods and the regal grandeur that they embodied. Housing over 20 Kushite kings, along with numerous queens and officials, these structures were not mere cenotaphs. Lavishly decorated burial chambers housed the royal personages, serving as their gateway to the afterlife, resplendent with their possessions for a life yet to begin anew.

7.1.2. Architecture and Significance

Unlike their Egyptian counterparts, the Nubian pyramids, humbler in their dimensions, were steeper, the inclination of their sides a sharp 70-degrees compared to the former's 50. The Kushite architecture was no less intricate, with detailed relief work, artefacts, and stylized, rectangular burial chambers. The sheer number of these structures - over 200, far surpasses the eighty or less on Egyptian soil, underlining the distinctive flavor of monumental architecture in the Kingdom of Kush.

7.2. Explorations and Excavations

Modern exploration of these pyramids began with the relentless endeavors of Swiss archaeologist George Andrew Reisner in the early 20th century. Braving immense adversities, he initiated the excavation of these structures, unveiling a string of secrets that would change our understanding of the Kingdom of Kush forever.

7.2.1. Reisner's Work

George Reisner, one of the first archaeologists to study the Sudanese pyramids, worked tirelessly to uncover the secrets of the ancients. Undeterred by perilous conditions and logistical difficulties, he made a series of groundbreaking discoveries. His tireless efforts unsealed the gateway into the mysterious royal tombs, artifacts, and the intricate assembly of the burial chambers, challenging previous notions about the Kingdom of Kush.

7.2.2. Further Excavations

Numerous subsequent excavations ensued, adding further dimensions to the enigma that is Nubia. The revelation of beautiful artifacts, amulets, impressive jewelry, royal regalia, statues of gods and goddesses, and stone inscriptions, drove home the narrative of a sophisticated, metropolis-like civilization, advanced in art, culture, script, and social strata. In recent years, multi-disciplinary approaches, employing technological advancements like Ground Penetrating Radar (GPR) and Hyper-spectral Imaging (HSI), have furthered our knowledge about these splendid creations of the past.

7.3. Looking Past the Sandstorms

The pages of history, dusted and adorned, have resurrected Nubia's lost civilization from its sandy shrouds, largely through the Pyramids of Sudan. Their presence echoes the tales of luxurious palaces, powerful monarchs, and a sophisticated lifestyle.

7.3.1. Defying Time and Nature

While decades of nature's harshness and human transgressions have chipped away at their grandeur, many of these edifices have remained partly intact. Even amid the volatile political climate and sporadic conflicts, the preservation of these pyramids is viewed as critical, reinforcing the importance of these architectural marvels in understanding a complex past.

7.3.2. Identity and Legacy

These pyramids, through their uncanny presence, continue to harbor the essence of the Kushite Kingdom. They embody the legacy left behind by this civilization, an identity etched into the stone and preserved within the folds of time. Projects allocating resources to conserve and restore these splendid remnants of history inch closer every day towards providing Sudan with the merited recognition as the land of Pyramids.

Before Egypt became a household name synonymous with pyramids, there existed the Kingdom of Kush, celebrating mortality with its monumental marvels. The Nubian pyramids today rise above the derisory monicker of 'poor cousins,' capturing imagination as towering emissaries of a past long lost, yet wrapped in layers of profound mystique, waiting to be unwrapped by the touch of time.

Chapter 8. Newgrange – Reviving Ireland's Ancient Astronomic Marvel

Nestled in the verdant landscape of Ireland's County Meath is a monument older than the Egyptian pyramids or Stonehenge. This prehistoric edifice known as Newgrange screams enigma from every inch of it, provoking awe among scholars, tourists, and locals alike.

8.1. The Discovery

In the summer of 1699, a local landowner, Charles Campbell, embarked on the extraction of stones from an intriguing mound on his property, utterly unaware of the historical wonder he was about to discover. Seeking material merely for building purposes, Campbell's workers chanced upon the entrance to the Newgrange passage tomb, laying bare secrets that had lain untouched for over 5,000 years. A significant sphere of archaeology emerged overnight, the mystical relic unleashing a narrative interwoven with ancient astronomy, mythology, and the mysteries of a long-lost civilization.

8.2. Description of the Monument

Newgrange is a colossal mound rising 40 feet off the ground and sprawling over an acre, encircled by a kerb of 97 hefty boulders. Its external beauty, an admixture of white quartz stones and rounded granite, is but a fascinating prologue to the treasures concealed within. A single narrow passage - 19 meters long and lined with large, engraved orthostat stones - leads to a cross-shaped chamber under the central mound. The innermost sanctum houses three alcoves, distinguished by large basin stones thought to host the ashes of the buried elite. The passage and chamber's walls are adorned with mysterious symbols thought to give a profound insight into the Bronze Age dwellers.

8.3. Astronomical and Mythological Significance

Newgrange, deemed the "Stone Age Cathedral," defies the paradigm of being a mere ancient tomb. Instead, this monument embraces its dual role as an astronomical marvel. Unraveling its celestial secret takes you to the Winter Solstice, when something magical transpires. An exact alignment of the tomb's entrance with the rising sun causes a beam of light to illuminate the 19-meter long passage and reach the inner chamber, a spectacle lasting a mere 17 minutes. This calculated, precise architecture points toward the advanced astronomical and mathematical capabilities of our pre-Celtic ancestors.

The Irish mythology, as chronicled in the "Book of Invasions," integrates Newgrange into its narrative, calling it Bru na Boinne. It is believed to be the home of the supernatural Tuatha de Danaan, specifically the Dagda, the father of the gods, and his son, the sun god Aengus.

8.4. Excavation and Preservation

The task of excavating and restoring Newgrange, along with preserving its archaeological integrity, was initiated in the 1960s under the leadership of Professor Michael J. O'Kelly of the University College, Cork. After meticulous excavation and conservation spanning over 14 years, Newgrange was opened to the public in 1975. In 1993, it achieved the coveted title of a UNESCO World Heritage site, highlighting its universal cultural significance.

8.5. Closing Thoughts

Newgrange stands as a testament to human resilience, curiosity and the primal need to understand and map the cosmos. It unravels a tale marked by brilliance and passion, pushing the boundaries of knowledge to comprehend the working of the cosmos and the cycle of life and death. With every visit, one is embraced by its enigmatic splendour, its stone whispers convincing you that the past is indeed intertwined with the present, as this ancient marvel continues to track the cosmos, just as it was designed thousands of years ago.

A visit to Newgrange, with its ancient charm and celestial connection, is a leap back to our ancestors' world, immersing us in a profound respect for their foresight and wisdom. Today, the monument stands not only as an emblem of Ireland's rich cultural and historical lineage but also as a beacon of humankind's undying fascination with life's mysteries—firmly rooting us in our shared past as we continue our journey into the future. Secure your copy of "Tales from the Crypts: Exploring the World's Hidden Tombs" and let us journey together through the annals of history, unravelling mysteries and capturing the essence of human determination and ingenuity.

Chapter 9. St.Peter's Tomb: A Journey Beneath the Vatican City

Nestled deep beneath the sprawling majesty of St. Peter's Basilica lies a world steeped in profound history and silent whispers from antiquity. A subterranean labyrinth, clad in dimly lit pathways and cobblestone corridors, it resonates with tales of a civilization lost in the sands of time. The beating heart of this architectural wonder, and perhaps the heart of Christianity itself, is St. Peter's Tomb.

9.1. The Invisible Basilica

The journey commences with the Necropolis - or city of the dead - a spectral edifice untouched by the wear of time. This haunting composition of crypts and mausoleums extends beneath the Vatican City, beckoning the curious to step into the shadows of the past. It was here, amidst grave markers scribed with archaic Latin and spectral frescos, that the tomb of St. Peter was discovered.

Long known as 'The Invisible Basilica', the Necropolis was sealed shut by Constantine the Great during the construction of the original St. Peter's Basilica in the 4th century AD. This act of preservation echoed across the ages, fortifying this cryptic space against the ravages of time. Millennia came and went, wars raged across lands and empires rose and fell, but the Necropolis remained, a silent guardian holding a secret in its formidable labyrinth.

9.2. The Excavations Unearthed

The modern narrative of St. Peter's Tomb began in the 20th century. When Pope Pius XI passed in 1939, his final wish was that his mortal remains find rest close to that of the principe degli apostoli, or Prince of the Apostles, Saint Peter. This request unravelled a tapestry of exploration and discovery.

A clandestine endeavor, spearheaded by Monsignor Ludwig Kaas in 1939, commenced the excavations. Archaeologists chiseled through layers of history, each stratum imbued with invaluable insights into Roman cultures and burial customs. When World War II's shadow darkened the world, the excavations did not cease. Instead, they transformed into a beacon of hope and unspoken tales of a civilization long lost but certainly not forgotten.

9.3. The Rediscovery

The moment of rediscovery arrived in 1941. As the archaeologists breached a wall, they stumbled on an ancient Roman pathway. The Red Wall complex, a layer of richly decorated memorials, proved a vision of death's grandeur in ancient Roman aristocratic traditions. But the mysterious Graffiti Wall with its encoded Christian symbols inscribed over hidden cavities of bones captivated researchers the most.

These were the unadorned tombs of the humble and the faithful, the final resting places of ordinary men and women who embraced Christian teachings when it was a fledgling faith. A fish, an age-old symbol of Christianity, and the Greek words "Petros Eni" – Peter is here – etched on the surface, suggested the presence of St. Peter's Tomb.

9.4. In the Shadow of the Pope

Unearthing St. Peter's Tomb was a feat of meticulous planning, careful execution, and hushed anticipation. Also known as the Field P, the area of the tomb held a hallowed silence, with every stone whispering tales of faith, sacrifice, and penance. An unassuming nook, veiled behind the Graffiti Wall, cradled a modest grave. Amid small bone fragments within, the excavators found an engraving on the wall — a triumphant invocation, "Peter is within."

For many researchers and archaeologists, this simple statement affirmed that they had indeed reached St. Peter's Tomb. However, for the devout, it was a celestial sign declaring the presence of the successor to Jesus Christ. Mirroring the words from Matthew 16:18, "You are Peter, and on this rock, I will build my Church", this humble locale beneath the Vatican City truly became the fundamental bedrock of the Roman Catholic Church.

9.5. Skeptics and Believers

The authenticity of the tomb and the bones within has sparked debates among skeptics and believers alike. In 1968, Pope Paul VI declared that the relics of St. Peter had been identified in a manner considered convincing. However, despite papal proclamation, doubts lingered among some historians and archaeologists.

Radiocarbon dating conducted in the early 21st century cast further doubts on the claim, placing the bones in the 1st century BC, which predated St. Peter. However, further examinations reflected the complex and overlapping nature of burial practices in the Necropolis.

9.6. A Symbol of Unwavering Faith

St. Peter's Tomb — a seemingly modest burial site, interwoven with cryptic entrances, carved inscriptions, and compact bone chambers — stands as an emblem of the profound enigma encircling Rome's underground. For believers, it's a symbol of unwavering faith; for historians, it's a window into a bygone era; for the Vatican City, it's a tribute of honor held in the heart of its foundation. The intertwining of faith and scientific exploration in the depths of this hallowed ground resonates with the enduring journey of mankind towards understanding its roots and origins.

The labyrinthine passages of the Vatican Necropolis continue to beckon curious souls, allured by the whispering echoes of the past. Despite the veil of mystery shrouding St. Peter's Tomb, the eternal beacon of faith it radiates remains undiminished, inviting us all on a timeless journey through the annals of our shared history.

Chapter 10. Taj Mahal: The Crypt of Eternal Love

Hidden in the heart of Agra, India, the gleaming monument of the Taj Mahal stands resplendent in all its marble glory - a poignant symbol of everlasting love and lament. The Taj Mahal, often lauded as a love letter written in stone, is a teardrop on the cheek of eternity. This monumental testament of a man's love for his wife invites us to peruse the crypt of eternal love.

10.1. Traversing Through Time

The Taj Mahal has a timeless appeal that transcends centuries, its pristine beauty unmatched and unparalleled. Built by the Mughal Emperor Shah Jahan in memory of his beloved wife, Mumtaz Mahal, the monument epitomizes the zenith of Mughal art and architecture.

Commissioned in 1632, it took over 21 years and 20,000 workers to construct this grand edifice. Craftsmen and artisans from as far as Turkey and Iraq were engaged in this mammoth project, ingraining the structure with a tapestry of diverse influences. The result is an astounding achievement of aesthetic and architectural genius.

10.2. The Man and His Muse

The love story of Shah Jahan and Mumtaz Mahal is steeped in romance and passion. Mumtaz, Shah Jahan's most cherished wife, stood by his side, providing counsel and companionship. When she passed away during childbirth, the heartbroken Emperor decided to immortalize their love within the epitome of splendor - the Taj Mahal.

Shah Jahan's grief was profound. His clothing turned white, his beard grew long, and his heart ached for his departed beloved. The Taj Mahal was his way to assuage the grief. The treasured tales of his longing ring down the annals of history, adding to the allure of this spectral monument.

10.3. A Masterpiece in Marble

The Taj Mahal evokes enchantment with its magnificent marbled exterior that sparkles in the sunlight and glows under the moon. The main dome, rising 44.4 meters high, is surrounded by four smaller domes. It embodies symmetrical perfection, with elegant minarets framing the central structure and gardens laying before it in perfect harmony.

The carvings on the Taj Mahal walls are another marvel. Intricate floral designs, delicate script motifs, and patterns bedeck the exterior. Calligraphy of Persian verses gives a sense of beatific serenity to this grand mausoleum.

Inside, the decoration becomes more elaborate. Incrusted with semi-precious stones, the cenotaph of Mumtaz Mahal is a sight to behold. It's worth noting that the cenotaphs inside the main chamber are merely for display. The actual graves, in adherence to Islamic law, are in a quieter, lower chamber.

10.4. The Crypt of Eternal Love

Shrouded in shadow and mystery lies the crypt of eternal love, a sanctum that reverberates with whispered prayers of undying love and echoes of a tale long lost in time. The crypt houses the cenotaphs of Shah Jahan and his beloved wife Mumtaz Mahal. Though visitors are not usually permitted to venture this far, the crypt remains an enigma, enveloped by an aura of mystic allure.

The heart of the Taj Mahal, this crypt, is a poignant testament to the love shared by Shah Jahan and Mumtaz Mahal. Against the backdrop of fine carvings and exquisite latticework, their cenotaphs lay side by side, stoic and silent. The sensation that fills the air here resembles standing at the precipice of a love so profound that it transcended death itself.

10.5. The Untamed Beauty of the Gardens

A stroll around the Taj Mahal's gardens offers a sense of tranquility that contrasts with the intricate, sculpted emotions of the monument itself. These gardens, simple in execution yet resonant in symbolism, embody paradise as depicted in the Quran.

These gardens represent a visual treat, converging in front of the monument in flawless symmetry. The central watercourse, reflecting the Taj's grandeur on its surface, further enhances the eternal charm of this everlasting love crypt.

10.6. A Love Story Engraved in Stone

The Taj Mahal is more than just a mausoleum – it's a testament of unyielding love, resounding through the ages with its legend. Behind the intricate carvings, under the colossal domes, beneath the eternally translucent marble, is a love story that refuses to be forgotten. Even after nearly four centuries, this symbol of eternal love continues to mesmerize, its enigmatic crypt a beacon of endless affection and undying devotion.

Among the world's crypts, the Taj Mahal remains unique, an ethereal monument of love and an enduring emblem of human passion, inviting visitors to step back in time, to explore its secret chambers, to experience its tale of eternal love. It's an invitation to unravel the mysteries of a love so intense that it defied mortality, and left its everlasting imprint on stone and time.

The Taj Mahal's enchantment, its ethereal beauty, and the crypt that bears the silent whispers of eternal love, offer a fascinating narrative that captivates the hearts of those who dare to delve into its wistful lore. This timeless marvel is a testament to the power of love and the human spirit's resilience, an ode to love etched in stone, frozen in time but echoing across eternity.

Chapter 11. The Capuchin Crypt: Rome's Chapel of Bones

Steeped in a silence that shatters the bustling hum of Rome's periphery, stands the Capuchin Crypt, a testament to time, mystery, and life beyond death. This crypt, beneath the site of the Santa Maria della Concezione dei Cappuccini, holds a fascination that transcends the ages, and it teases the delicate boundary between the macabre and the devout.

11.1. Origins and Construction

Around 1631, the Capuchin friars, members of the Order of Friars Minor Capuchin, an offshoot of the Franciscan Order, made their move from the friary at St. Bonaventure to their new home at Santa Maria della Concezione. The relocation saw the accompanied transport of 300 cartloads of deceased friars' remains, excavated from the friary's soil. The idea, profoundly spiritual, was to let none of their brethren be forgotten on their transcendent journey.

The bones were painstakingly arranged to adorn the multiple chapels within the crypt. An ornate spectacle of skeletal remains now bore an artistic yet eerie presentation, offering a tangible connection to the eternal, a bridge between life and death, and an unspoken lesson on the transient nature of earthly existence.

11.2. Design and Decorum

The crypt is divided into five chapels, each ornately decorated and curated with skeletal remains — The Crypt of the Resurrection, Mass Chapel, Crypt of the Skulls, Crypt of the Pelvises, and Crypt of the Leg

Bones and Thigh Bones. Remarkably, each one serves its purpose, honoring an aspect of the friars' journey while meditating on the concept of life's impermanence.

The Crypt of the Resurrection, adorned with a skeleton encrusted in dried roses, symbolizes the resurrection in Christian theology. As visitors venture further, the Mass Chapel, bereft of bones, houses a functional altar with the relics of martyrs St. Urbain and St. Valentin. Frescoed scenes from the life of St. Francis of Assisi grace the chapel walls, infusing the crypt with poignant religious symbolism.

Next, the Crypt of the Skulls, and the Crypt of the Pelvises offer a stark illustration of the bodies' frailty and transient nature in their purest form. Here, Capuchin friars utilized skulls and pelvises to create delicate patterns, erecting arches and crosses, and creating an ambience that resonates simultaneously with fascination, horror, and strangely, peace.

Finally, the Crypt of the Leg Bones and Thigh Bones serves as the last chapel. Here, the sight of the meticulously arranged leg bones and thigh bones is a reminder of humankind's mortality and imperfections, creating a hallowed space for contemplation.

11.3. Reflections on Life and Death

What might seem an eclectic spectacle of the grotesque is, in reality, the Capuchin friars' philosophically profound perspective on the cycle of life and death. The crypt, cloaked in solemn silence and adorned with the relics of 4,000 friars, whispers a message of life's ephemeral nature and reminds passersby of the eternal reality waiting for mortal beings.

Far from being a macabre spectacle intended to provoke fear, the crypt is a silent sermon on life's uncertainty. A reminder that physical beauty is fleeting, and even in death, humans can impart a message, make their presence felt, and leave behind a legacy that transcends the physical form. In this light, the arrangement of the bones capitalizes on death's universality and the constant presence of our mortality.

11.4. Contemporary Reverence

With each year, the Capuchin Crypt continues to draw visitors from all walks of life, bringing together historians, believers, skeptics, and everyone in between. Its darkness holds an uncanny attraction, and the grim yet fascinating surroundings intrigue the modern mind, raising questions about life, death, and the hereafter.

The crypt is more than just a morbid curiosity; it invites introspection, much in the spirit of a memento mori — a reminder of mortality — and beckons you to explore its depths physically and metaphorically. Even as the sun sets and the city's sounds muffle into the night, the crypt stands, a silent sentinel, holding within its hollowed chambers the tales of the dead, waiting to be heard, remembered, and carried on through the whisperings of time.

In the hushed confines of the Capuchin Crypt, the bone-chapel of Rome, the past intertwines with the present, mystery shrouding each skeletal artefact. Its very existence, teetering on the edge of eerie fascination and profound lesson, enshrines the Capuchin friars' belief in life's fleeting nature and the inevitability of death, leaving an indelible mark on all who bear witness.